Johanna Sparrow

Black Blood

How to Combat Racism and End the Public Execution of Black Life

Johanna Sparrow

Johanna Sparrow

DEDICATION

To those who strive for constant progression

Johanna Sparrow

<u>ACKNOWLEDGMENTS</u>

Thanks to my editor and family

Johanna Sparrow

CONTENTS

INTRODUCTION

A black plague has landed on the doorsteps of low income black neighborhoods, and black men have been the major targets. Our black men's blood is quickly filling the streets around the world, while the screams of their loved ones echo across every social media and news broadcast. Black executions aren't hidden. They're openly laid out to provoke even the most peaceful soul to rage. Isn't that the plan? A true hunter baits his prey into attacking him so the kill can be justified when it was a planned execution all along. It's as if white men await in the shadows for black blood.

The truth is being exposed, no matter how raw, uncut, and cold-hearted it is. Black men are being hunted down and executed regularly by overly eager cops who enjoy the hunt and kill of black life. What are we missing here? Why can't we see this? Who truly gives a damn about black life? These cowards and racists have aligned and joined forces. Not against true crime, but against you, my black brother and sister, and we're too damn distracted amid our demise to educate ourselves on how to combat it.

Who ushered in this black plague? Has it always been here, but hidden in plain sight. Has it been dressed up to give us the false belief that we're protected when we're actually being put to death? And the genius part of it all is that they've created a war between black people, which has allowed the hunter to set up camp in our neighborhoods and place us under siege to cruel and ravishing destruction.

A traffic stop should never be the last stop of your life. It's becoming increasingly unsafe to be a black male in the United States. But eventually, the shedding of black blood will backfire and create unity amongst the people.

CHAPTER ONE

A CALL TO ACTION

There's still so much that needs to be done to stop the slaughtering of black lives, but are we really looking at the complete problem, or are we placing blame where we see fit? Something is terribly wrong, and there's not one specific reason why we're seeing so many killings in our neighborhoods and communities. Are we the only race whose youth are facing annihilation? Are we too weak and afraid to act on our anger? Why is it that other races can express their pain and rage when their youth are murdered without warrant by white police, but we're criticized if we roll our eyes?

We show strength, but in the wrong areas. When young people took the streets in protest of the recent killings by the hands of white police officers, there was a clash between the younger and older generations. What I saw was the youth crying out for something to be done, knowing that a quiet and peaceful march is outdated and that it isn't going to solve the attacks on the black community. The youths didn't hold back their emotions. They used their anger and marched with passion in an attempt to force change.

Sure, their behavior was unruly and out of control, but how else was the world going to hear them? How else were they going to get the attention of the world's eye to say *enough is enough* and *I don't want to be next*? The march didn't only include black youths, but people from all cultures who understood that the violent attacks on black youth needs to stop. To say that *black lives matter* is unnecessary because it's innately understood. And to counter with *all lives matter* shows the blatant disregard and disrespect that white people have for black people's suffering by their hands. They don't want to admit all the unfair advantages they receive from the system of white supremacy.

Yes, the black lives that have been snuffed out because of hate didn't matter to those white police officers. But if we are to really deal with the root of the issue, we have to bring to light that black lives are taken every day by black people. The truth is that black lives matter every day, and not just on the days when we're killed by a white person! How do you get a group of people to see that every day is a fight and a battle for black life? Many times, we don't confront the demons within our own culture, but we're eager to confront it elsewhere. This way of handling things isn't going to stop the terror in our communities. No matter how much we march, pump our fists, and sing, we'll still be forced to deal with the truth of having to take responsibility for our self-hate in order to end the madness.

I remember hearing a few of my loved ones talking about the order of things in the world and how the black community is the scapegoat for people's feelings. I know it's bold to say, but all we have to do is take an honest look at how misguided our young people have become, and think about how they became that way because they didn't raise themselves. If there's a chain reaction in the wake of violence on black life that was set off by war within black communities, we must take some accountability.

Below are the seven qualities that will end black-on-black destruction:

- Accountability

- Awareness

- Forgiveness

- Love

- Respect

- Responsibility

- Understanding

Until we understand how to incorporate these qualities into our daily lives, we'll continue to be prey to infiltration and violence. This has gone on long enough, and now, the final outcome hangs in the balance, and our mentality and attitudes will determine the amount of black blood that continues to be spilled around the world.

If you think everything that's going on around you is unreal, you're only deceiving yourself into thinking everything is fine. Can't you see that you've been hit with guilt by association due to common ground, race, and culture? You're not going to escape the effects of racism no matter how much money or status you have. Our neighborhoods

are warring with each other while our youth are

ducking bullets, and the elderly are being abused. It

sickens me that we've become blind to the truth

because of the hate we have for each other.

That hate is just one more thing that has the

world distracted about who we really are. We need

a call to action that begins with accountability. We

all want the chaos that affects us to cease. For that

to happen, we must do something about it as a

collective, but it starts with each individual making

positive changes in their daily lives.

We must accept that we've subconsciously

accepted the degrading labels that society has

placed on us, and it shows through our behavior.

Until we reverse this, we'll continue to see killings

in our own backyards, and we'll be helpless to stop them. How can I take accountability for something that's done to me? Why should I be the one taking the blame? I'm speaking about us coming into the knowledge of how much power we truly have, and we can access that power by standing together. We've been conquered for so long because we have chosen to be divided on issues such as religion, status, politics, and skin tone. Many killings that take place in our communities are by our own hands over silliness like video games, shoes, or clothing, but we're mostly made aware of police officers taking our lives during traffic stops.

Below is a list of what black people must take accountability for:

- Chasing fame and wealth instead of health and knowledge.

- Forsaking our elderly and mistreating our young.

- Individualistic mindset instead of sticking together and spending money within our own community.

- Killing someone who looks like us without a hesitation, but won't even speak out against the real enemy.

- Leaving young people behind, because of jail time or drugs, to raise themselves.

- Morally misguided.

- Trading love, knowledge, and spirituality for technology. As a result, we're fearful, anxious, dependent, and intellectually disabled.

- Lacking the knowledge and spiritual wisdom that would enable us to change our mentality, and therefore, change our situation.

- We're often tired from being over-worked and disrespected by everyone, including our own people, and we react like animals toward our spouses and children as a result.

- Reaching a certain monetary status and separating ourselves from our own people instead of giving back.

In order to create change, you have to admit your part in the problem and change your perception of your capabilities and potential. If we can all accept responsibility, we can begin the process of change within our own communities. The world's perception of you won't change until you first change how you think of yourself.

Our communities have been taken over by bullies and war lords. Therefore, we aren't only being attacked externally by the police. We're also being attacked by our own children, which tells the world that we don't value our own lives and that it's okay to kill us at will because we act like savages. Instead of ignoring the truth, we should accept the challenges we face and get back to being the kings and queens that we truly are.

Below is a list of things we need to take responsibility for:

- Allowing our young men and women to be murdered in large numbers.

- Fearing our own people.

- Lacking patience and always looking for instant gratification taking actions that will reap benefits 10, 30, 50 years in the future.

- Lack of fathers in the home.

- Lack of exemplary educational opportunities for young people.

- Not helping our young people to understand accountability and responsibility.

- Playing into the stereotypes that white people have labelled us with.

- Trying to get away from our own people as soon as possible to move into white neighborhoods.

The road ahead of us is unclear for many reasons. The call to action is to come together and move beyond survival mode, and determine how we can thrive and excel. Organization is what we lack. We can't continue to rely solely on individual abilities. We must to use our voices, knowledge, and business acumen as a collective.

We've done that before in the 1920s when we had our own businesses, banks, and law enforcement—Black Wall Street. The only hate and that threatened us was outside our community, and we thrived. Now, we don't know what it's like to work together, and the individualistic mindset is dangerous. Can we make a difference in the lives of other black people? The answer is yes, as long as we're building ourselves up from within and not seeking for our oppressor to solve our community issues.

We're not properly parenting our youth. We have young people being kicked out of their homes or leaving home and not being allowed to come back. What's up with that? The most loving and understanding people have become the most savage and destructive—titles that've been given to us for years, and we're acting this way daily. We don't have a vision of where we're going or where we want to go because we have no guidance or direction. Other races play on that and use it against us. Our own foolishness, insecurity, ignorance, and poverty consciousness makes us look upon the most savage people as kind and loving and look to them for help.

Can we all do more to change how we see ourselves and each other within our communities? Are we still going to play this childish game of chaos while everyone takes shots at us? What's clear is that we aren't willing to analyze the truth. We'd rather point fingers and place blame on anyone besides ourselves. I'm sorry if you didn't get the memo, but this battle includes you also. Even if you refuse to act, your lack of concern will have a devastating outcome. We all must come together to save the community. We either stand together to change our reality, behaviors, and perspective, or we'll be destroyed. The lack of awareness that we possess is the ignorance that's allowing our neighborhoods to be ravished.

Below is a list of qualities that are present when people possess awareness:

- Ability to use intellect and reason.

- Live in communities, which consists of owning your own banks, schools, business, and police force, as opposed to neighborhoods.

- Knowledge of self.

- Knowledge of who wants to destroy you.

- Self-love.

- Unselfishness. Sharing knowledge and wealth.

- Wisdom, discernment, and good judgement

These are just a few things that will create a better environment. I know that race shouldn't be the defining factor of how we treat each other, but it is in this society, and we need to play the game correctly to be successful.

How can we challenge how other races view us when we still argue amongst ourselves and show each other hate? We don't listen to each other because of differing religions or political views. There are many outcomes available to us, but the outcomes we chose will be based on our level of responsibility, awareness, knowledge, and understanding. The truth is that we're trying to look at the world as one people when we don't even treat each other as one. I challenge you to do something where ever you are.

Why are we teaching our young men to respect filthy police, to run when they're innocent, and to fight instead of using their minds to settle disagreements? As we're tired of our own people who won't do what's right, we're also fed up with those ignorant mindsets as well. White supremacy wants you to think and act only for the benefit of you as an individual, while at the same time, associating the actions of one black person with the entire group. This mind game is played around the world. This is what keeps young black men as targets of public execution. Getting others to see the black community as a people who stand together rather than kill is going to take a collective effort from us all. Men and women need to participate in shifting the way we see ourselves. I'm not your enemy, so stop believing that I am. We've bought into these roles and acted like savages for so long that the world has grown tired of our existence.

Now that you understand what has to be done to break the psychological hold that has been placed on black people, we can make progress in cleaning up the mess we've made. At this stage, it doesn't matter who implanted thoughts of self-hate in us or what has caused the evil of mass killings on blacks. Now we need to take action that will create changes in our mindset and how we view each other. We must remove the blood from our own hands if we want to stop being killed by white people. We must stop mistreating each other if we want others to stop mistreating us. Yes, blood is on our hands for the amount of lives we take within our own communities without contemplation. We'll continue to lose the battle against the public executions of our people if we don't stop killing each other in the streets. Many people in the black community don't care, so why should anyone else?

Many of us are so stubborn that we turn a blind eye to what's really happening because of our only-do-for-self mentality, while our youth are needlessly dying due to manipulation and mind control. When we all learn to take responsibility and start thinking like intelligent beings, we'll gain control of our homes, schools, and communities.

Let's stop allowing our youth to be disciplined by

someone who doesn't want to protect us because of

their racist views.

What are you going to do about the crime in

black neighborhoods? Why can't we come together

to stop the violence without looking for a racist,

hateful people to rescue us? We've repeatedly seen

law enforcement's mistreatment of us because of

how they think of us, yet we continue to depend on

them to discipline our children and validate our

existence. Wake the hell up!

When you think about how we ask outsiders to

regulate our neighborhoods, it's no wonder why the

crime rate is so high. You can't expect someone that

doesn't understand you and that doesn't *want* to

understand you to protect you or act in behalf of your best interest. When you depend on your own people to help you spark change without the aid of your oppressor, you'll then rid the need for police to protect your neighborhoods. If they're not in your neighborhoods, then they can't mistreat and abuse you. You have the power to make these changes, but it will take intelligent, mature, and unity-based thinking to do so.

CHAPTER TWO

BLACK BLOOD

I love you even though I don't know you and have never ever seen you. I love you because you're a product of me—a life that deserves respect, protection, and love. It breaks my heart to see you being killed in the streets. I'm talking to you, black man. I love you, and I'm very tired of what's happening to you. What can I do to help you? Please tell me how I can make this sickness to stop? How long has law enforcement been hurting you when they're supposed to protect and serve you?

I never thought that in 2018, we'd still be seeing these race-based killings flashed across every news channel. And many people condemn what's taking place in third world countries as the same things occur in their own backyard. For the African-American male, his life doesn't seem to be worthy to white America unless he bleeds his black blood. Why are my men still being sacrificed in front of the world? This doesn't mean that other cultures aren't experiencing the same injustices, but black males are affected at a disproportionate rate. It feels like it's open season on black men, and it terrifies me because I have a son. I have a front row ticket to the demise of the black male. Even after black people have been fighting so long for peace and equality, I'm still forced to watch you get abused in the streets.

The pain in the black community is real, and although I don't know every black male that has lost their life to police brutality, that doesn't stop the heartbreak and burning in my soul. I scream internally for the killing of my black men to stop. Has the law enforcement in every state declared war on the black male? This problem isn't close to being solved, and every law enforcement department needs to be investigated to make sure they're comprised of officers that want to protect everyone equally. The black man's blood has put a black mark on this planet through the constant slaughtering and sacrificing of their lives. What can we do as a collective to stop this horrific and unjust behavior?

Below is a list of things we can do to end police brutality:

- Create organizations in every state that focus on exposing police killings of unarmed black people.

- Form organizations that protect our neighborhoods and towns, and stop depending on law enforcement to protect us.

- Realize that racism isn't dead just because we have a black president, and act according to that awareness.

- Unite to continue the preaching of equal love, respect, and justice for all of humans.

My heart is constantly bruised over the treatment and continuous killing of black men. Not only am I a mother of a son, but I'm also the sister of many brothers, so I'm very devastated over your loss. I feel the pain you experience from being treated unjustly. The world doesn't see the greatness that I see in you, and no matter what you've done, you should be treated fairly. I hear your cries, and I'm sorry for what you've had to endure. Even though it's difficult, forgive those that mistreat you. Harboring hate and anger only hurts you, and not the person you're hating. To think clearly and to properly plan the steps to freedom, you must forgive and let go of over-emotionality. Your black blood won't go unnoticed. Your loss won't be silenced because the manner in which you've behaved in the face of tragedy has shown the world who you really are—light and love!

They've tried to silence your voice, and if you smile or show any signs of comfortability, you're reminded that you're not welcomed through hate and violence. You may think that it'll never happen to you, but we all see how real the war is that has been waged against you. They want your black blood in the streets and your murders broadcast on every media network. I refuse to remain silent over the spilling of your black blood. I'll never forget, and I won't let your deaths be treated as insignificant.

CHAPTER THREE

NO JUSTICE, NO PEACE

Is there really such a thing as blind justice? I'm starting to see clearly and that the meaning of justice depends on your prospective. You deserve justice when your life is taken prematurely and unjustly. And although many don't see the value of your existence, I do. I understood how you feel. It's written all over your face that you feel insignificant and hopeless when you're taken away in the back of a police car. Your eyes say, *I won't be back,* yet we watch you die for insignificant reasons and do nothing about it. We march, shout, and cry, but the killings haven't stopped.

I know you're tired, yet we remain apathetic as the system of white supremacy labels you as criminal, unruly, and dangerous so the world can be desensitized to your slaughter and destruction. It just isn't fair, and I'm shouting it to the top of my lungs as I pen this to you. I wish I could change what's going on and wipe your slate clean, because you don't deserve to be treated like this. You're not an enemy of this world. I'm so in love with you, and your death leaves me crushed. I must heal my heart so I can use my voice and gifts, to help rescue you out of this mental and emotional prison called reality.

How the world views you is unwarranted. When you bleed, your pain is felt by us all. We must become stronger as a people and stop hiding behind the fear of death so we can garner the courage to stand up to our oppressor. Your death is constantly discussed, but no one talks about your greatness and potential. Oh God! Why have you forsaken us as a people, and what must we do to stop this abuse so that the world can see the true beauty of the black man and woman without the unjust fear that created by a society to keep black blood pouring in the streets?

Below is a list of how black men have been treated unjustly:

- Lengthy prison sentences for lesser crimes.

- Murdered when unarmed.

- Murdered in public.

- White people that murder black people serve minimal jail time, if any at all.

Not everyone is looking the other way. Many people are coming together for your black blood. As this continues to happen, the rest of the world must take notice. The disproportionate unfair treatment of one race must stop! The world won't continue to remain silent over this issue. All life is precious, and should be treated as such.

The black man's life has been marked for slaughter. As much as people from all walks of life are coming together in one voice, the cry is still unheard by white supremist. But we must reach them if there's going to be real justice. Who are the real criminals here? What I've learned is that a people who 've been bullied and slaughtered for generations, stop fearing death, and they become powerful as a result.

This isn't the world we want to continue to exist in. The marches and cries won't stop until every life has been accounted for and the slaughtering of the black male stops. How many will continue to stand with us and relinquish fear of the powers that be? I'm prepared to fight for your life and the future of my seed. With so much hurt and pain going on in the world, including war and terrorism, why is our country waging war on black men? These are the same black lives that it will ask to help fight a foreign enemy. When we wake up and realize how the killing of black men affects everyone, we'll be able to stop it. We must stop ignoring the fact that our children are murdered daily, and decide to take a stand.

CHAPTER FOUR

PUBLIC EXECUTION

I've seen what they've done to you in public and behind closed doors. It's unjust. Why can't you be given a fair trial like everyone else? Is it because your public execution and black blood brings happiness to many? You shouldn't have to worry about being executed and disrespected before the world. Wake up black man and show the world that your life is valuable. For without you, the black woman couldn't reproduce your glory.

I'm sickened by your abuse. Your life is just as

precious and worthy as anyone else's. How long have you been bleeding while we all looked the other way? Now the veil is being removed with each killing. Each murder leaves a bruise on the black community. Is the black man not human in the eyes of the rest of the world? Why is he being repeatedly paraded about for the amusement of white people? These killings won't go unpunished, and justice will be served in due time. Until then, every human being must refuse to turn away because it could be your child, father, or husband that's victimized next.

Universal justice will take center stage soon, and all will watch in horror. It doesn't matter if you believe in a higher power or not. The universe has a way of making things right for all. Until then, the black man's story will never be forgotten, and I'll never turn a blind eye to your peril. The world now sees how racism has caused your struggle more than ever. I see the hurt and pain in your families' eyes and hear a deafening cry in their voices when they speak your name. I've been moved to tell those who love you that I'm deeply sorry. My sorrow is for the never-ending brutality you face and that my own children and grandchildren are doomed to face.

There's just no way to deal with this other than out in the open where everyone can witness your death at the hands of racist white men. We're all shocked by the executions and tortures that take place in other countries, yet we watch silently at the beating and murdering of black men in America. We choose to see no resemblance to the same cruelty that takes place abroad. I'm certain that I'm not the only one who's sick of this war on black people. And many will try to argue that it's not just black men that are dying at the hands of law enforcement, but people of all races. While that may be true, the death of black men is constantly showed on every news channel. Is this a method to keep the black community in fear?

Today, you can't turn on the television without seeing the breaking news of another black male being shot down while crowds of people protest, "Black lives matter." How many more black men do we have to lose before something significant is done? How many more lives do we have to endure before the murderers are brought to justice and held accountable for their actions. Why is it that those senseless murders are always done by whites? Do they have a subconscious fear of the black man that causes them to shoot first and ask questions later? Is it all about the news stations getting more ratings by showing the overabundance of the loss of black life?

Below is a list of reasons that underlie public

executions:

Bullying a certain race because of prejudices.

Control over a race to commit genocide.

Planting evidence to kill at will.

The destruction of a race's character to justify killing them.

To instill fear in group of people that they innately fear.

No matter how loud you scream *black lives matter*, you must look within to understand what's really taking place in the world we live in. Are we really sitting on the banks of unacknowledged slavery and killed for our skin color? As much as I would like to say no, I can't. We are indeed looking at the twisted and perverted form of justifiable homicide on a people that most of the world would like to call dead. But are we dead?

Today, my son must run for his life from the same people he's taught to respect. He must live in a world where trust doesn't exist because of the color of his skin. Now tell me, who's inhumane? I can only tell you what I see or what the world wants me to see. While war is taking place all around us and terror can end up on your doorstep because of your beliefs, we have a gang of men outside the black community that are purging who they feel is their biggest threat—the black man. Now, black women are left to protect their black children against the evils of the world.

Everyone can see our communities drying up and our young people leaving, if not dying, but still no one cares. Why is it that when a black life is taken, there's a negative story of that person's life displayed on every TV network and social media avenue as if to justify the murder of that black person? Why do we only care when we're watching our youth gunned down in the streets

like animals? Are we that desensitized that we don't feel

a damn thing about it except when we're forced to?

CHAPTER FIVE
A MOTHER'S TEARS

The weeping of a mother who's lost a child will bring sympathy to the hearts of anyone that hears her cries. In the black community, mothers are losing their children every day to violence at the hands of law enforcement. When did a black man's life become so expendable and considered collateral damage? It seems that lately, black men's lives are being challenged by more than just neighborhood violence or racial experimentation, but something more sinister to combat the positive image of a

black man as the President.

Why is it that the life of the black man isn't

valued or seen as equal to every other man on the

planet? When will this war on the black lives stop?

How many more black mothers must cry or lose a

son before the violence against the black man's life

ends? The presence of a black man in the White

House has brought on even more hatred against

black men, and the success of any black man creates

a need for white supremists to create more

punishment for black success.

What a crazy world we live in knowing that

mothers are crying over the loss of their children's

lives, not because he committed a crime, but

because of the color of his skin. While many people

in the world want to have some color in their skin, the ones who have it naturally are murdered because of it. Having so many brothers of my own kept me praying for their safety every time they walked out the door. As a mother of a son, a daughter, and the wife of a black man, my concern is no different from my mother's for her sons, which is for them to make it home at the end of the day. Yes, mothers of all walks of life lose sons because of violence, but black men are killed at a much higher rate.

Are the tears of black mothers not important enough to stop the killings that are constantly taking place? Are the tears of a black mother any less deserving of understanding the worry and pain she endures daily? Why is the black male's death continuously flashed across our screens? When will her tears stop so she can smile again? Why do black women suffer and bury more of their children than mothers of any other race? Why is the world hating and killing people for something they are dying to have—melanin? How many more of our sons will black people be forced to bury?

Does this sound extreme that I'm focusing on the black male's death and his mother's tears? Are we all so blind that we can't see that the issues that many white people have with any black man in power. With the success of any black man comes a price to be paid by poor, underprivileged black people. Sure, many of our young men are dying at the hands of their own, but they're also being disproportionately murdered at hands of our enemy in broad daylight. Why are we sitting back watching our young black men get picked off for target practice? Why can't our voices stop this madness? Is it because the hate is so deep-rooted that we must dig deep to the root of the matter to solve it? How many young, white youth have you seen shot down by black police officers? How many Asians have you seen gunned down? This is more than just senseless killings. It was the hateful white supremacists' way of saying, "We can do whatever we want to you while the President is black, and wealthy black people that can make a difference will only sit back and watch." Did anyone else receive this message?

Didn't you think because you had a black president that you were going to be helped. Did you think that he was going to stop what's going on?

When will this madness end? The worst part of all this is that many of these poor black communities are helping the public's judgement of the black man by killing black people themselves. How long will our people scream, *no justice, no peace*? The tears of the black woman should've stopped a long time ago, but they haven't. In fact, they've doubled in the past seven years, and we can only imagine why. When will I stop seeing the tears of the black mother crying over the death of her sons? She's no different from any other mother in that she loves and cares for her children just as deeply.

Below are the effects that the death of a child has on a family:

- Anger

- Bitterness

- Confusion

- Depression

- Fear

- Grief

- Health depletion

- Insomnia

- Rage

Experiencing the murder of your child is a pain that can't be explained, yet African-Americans deal with it every day. The only way to stop the bloodshed and suffering is to stand up and do something about it. We must rally together to stop the assassinations of our black men in particular.

How long are we going to be a scattered people that are divided amongst each other? We can't stand together for any common good, and we've learned to trust our oppressor before we trust each other. How on earth are we going to stop the slaughter of our people if we can't trust and love each other and work together? Mothers need to come together in every neighborhood, not just when they lose a child, but well before that to prevent death. We must work together to let each young adult know that they're loved and that they have the ability to build a strong and safe community. The question is, how many mothers are willing to do this without having experienced the death of a child? How many mothers are fighting to make a difference in their neighborhoods?

Mothers should be enjoying life while peacefully watching their children grow up with a bright future. They shouldn't have to worry about whether their child will make it home safely because they can easily be a target due to their skin color. For all the mothers who've lost a child, know that your tears aren't in vain. The black community will rise up one day to protect our people.

CHAPTER SIX

WAKE UP!

When will the black community wake up from sleeping while their neighborhoods are destroyed by terrorist acts from white people who fear them? We aren't just under attack by other culture, but often, we're attacked by our own children who've made the decision to pick up arms against his or her fellow man. We hear the call to wake up all over black communities, but how many of us take heed?

We point fingers and blame each other for the problems within our culture, and when we seek change, we look for help from people and organizations outside of our communities.

We've become such a broken people that we fail to see how much we've been divided. But we're the only ones that can truly look after ourselves. If you can't stand side by side with people who look like you and live in the same environment as you to foster change, then how will you ever get out the predicament you're in? When we all come to our senses is when we can create real change, but until then, we're forced to live in a world where we're at the mercy of any outsider that wants to attack us. Until we can stop fighting each other, nothing will change. If we can't envision how we can work together to keep our neighborhoods safe, our mothers and fathers will continue burying their children. Funny how we take everyone else's side when it comes to standing for something, yet we can't stand with each other.

Who has caused us to hate each other? Who has sold us the false reality that disowning our own is beneficial? I see the effects of this mindset every day, and it sickens me to see how we'd rather complain and argue over meaningless things instead of working together to keep our families and neighborhoods safe. I've learned that if someone can keep you distracted, they can do anything that they want to you. Have you looked in the mirror lately? What did you seen that needs to be changed? Waking up doesn't mean that you should physically destroy your enemy. It means you need to change your thinking patterns. You need to alter how you view yourself, and others will change how they treat you as a result. My prayer is that we wake up and return to the place where we understood each other, trusted each other, and had each other's backs no matter what white people thought of us. Until we stop trying to identify with every other racial group except black, we won't know who we are or our purpose.

How can you be my enemy? Who has given me that concept to not trust you in business or any other aspect of life? Why is this just a black problem? As much as you realize that you're black, you try even harder not to be associated with anything black. I've never seen a people who run from their identity as much as black people. These are broken people that don't know themselves or their history before slavery. If I don't love myself, then how can I expect someone else to love me? Before we can stop what someone else is doing, we must change our mentality and perspective on what it means to be black.

Are you just surviving instead of living? Are you only ducking your head to avoid trouble from white people? Why can't you muster the courage to help your community? I'm not here to tear you down, but get you to wake up and start speaking up for your human rights. Do you care about what's going on in your neighborhood and how the young are dying before the old? Aren't you concerned about the genocidal plot on black people? Are you even aware of it? How quick we are to forgive others, but we'll shoot a black person quickly for looking at us the wrong way? How quick we are to show the world that we're a forgiving people, yet our neighborhoods and communities are saturated with the stench of death? Do you truly think we can come out of this by attacking each other?

I'd like to see a better quality of living for my people. I want us to be strong and powerful in numbers and change how we treat each other. We must stop seeing ourselves as criminals and feeling as if no one loves us. We must show love for ourselves and each other. We've waged war on ourselves while being played like pawns in a chess game, waiting for the real opponent's next move. Foolish people we are that refuse to open our eyes to our own destruction. Our ignorant behavior causes death, but we act as if we can't see it. Why are we so cruel to each other? How can you not see that you're only hurting yourself and your people?

Always making it known to the world that we love all people, but afraid to say that we love black people. No other race has that issue. We have a sick mentality, which is why we are a sick people. You must love yourself and people who look like you before you can love anyone else. We take on battles for every other cause and wonder why people in our communities are dying at an exorbitant rate. So many of our people have emotionally left our communities. So many have distanced their hearts because they see no good in us. How many people are around afraid to say something because they don't know if they'll be a target if they do speak up?

How many of us choose violence instead of peace while looking for respect from others when you're unwilling to give it? Are we so sick that the entire world looks down on our black faces in pity? Wake up from the slumber of death you're in. Wake up from the ignorance that blinds you from the truth. We've become an abandoned village. Our young people have taken up arms against us, and others have moved into white neighborhoods because they don't trust their own people. No matter how many times we shake our heads in disgust at the loss of life, we play a role in our demise by remaining silent. Our people have been abandoned by not only the system of racism white supremacy that seeks to destroy us, but also their own people who see no good in them. We all must be held accountable for the role we play or don't play in making positive changes in our communities. Fathers, why have your sons forgotten you and your historical struggles? Mothers, why do your daughters refuse to listen your words of wisdom? Why, because they see the double-mindedness that we have. We talk like we want to be strong and consistent, but we've actually become a race of followers with no backbone that fears the white man.

Wake up and hear the many cries of abandoned black babies in the foster care system who now suffer broken hearts. What about the dozens of young women that desperately search for love, only to find disrespect because they have no protection from their fathers? So you think you can just run to another race and forget the problems of the race you were born into? When something bad happens by the hands of a black person that you're associated with, you're going to be treated as a black person. Still, you disown your own people. For what? Where has that gotten you? Instead of running away from issues, know yourself and help your people. Do something that at least sparks change.

Below is a list of ways you can begin to make a difference:

- Gain knowledge of how you can create change and share those tools with others.

- Gain knowledge of self and teach that truth to those that have ears to hear.

- Realize that life is more than sports and spending money. Help others cultivate their gifts and use them to benefit the world.

- Stop attacking others for their lack of knowledge and help them gain the knowledge that you have.

- Stop the violence, and instead, use your mind to create and innovate. Put your ideas to use within your community.

Too many times, we see our people from the perspective of white society, which is often not a positive light. Young black men are being executed daily at high rates, and all we do is sing songs and march. Fighting for change means more than marching. We must work together to fix our problems. While divided, we'll never overcome or make progress. I only want to see positive changes take place, and for those changes to occur within our communities, they must first take place within each individual. How do you change the views of a people when every media outlet subliminally sends a message to the entire world that black is bad? Are you playing into the beliefs of white people to get a piece of the pie?

Stop being distracted from the slaughter of your people. You could be next. No matter how much you try to make them feel comfortable by relaxing your hair, lightening your skin, or making your voice higher, they still see you as a nigger and a threat to their genetic survival. The best thing you can do for yourself is to know yourself and love yourself. Don't worry about what anyone else thinks about you. No one can stop you from succeeding but yourself, so don't give anyone else that power, even if they have a system behind them. What God has for you is for you, and no one can take it away. This is your wake-up call to go forth and be great despite the odds that may be against you. Let those odds make you stronger, smarter, and propel you to even greater success. Wake up!

CHAPTER SEVEN

DISBELIEF

How many times have you awakened to the news of a shooting that resulted in the loss of a black life? The knowledge that black life doesn't matter to many people is often displayed in the media where citizens march, ask for peace, and protest for police to stop killing innocent black victims. Why hasn't white society taken heed to the call to disarm and decided to work together to bring about peace? Why does it seem that for every non-black life that's taken, two to three black people are killed, and those killings are broadcasted? There's something seriously wrong with that picture. The fact that a black life can be taken when they have no weapon and that there are often no repercussions for the offenders, blows my mind.

The tactics used to put fear in a certain race for control purposes is still happening today. When will the unwarranted murders of black men cease and justice take its place? I can't imagine what the generations before us went through and how they survived those times. What should a mother do when her child leaves the house and she doesn't know if he or she will return? Should she live a life of fear for her child's existence? Why is this only the case for black people? Amid all this, black people still refuse to see each other as brother and sister, and instead, we try our best to identify with someone else's culture. What will it take for my people to see that we have a severe problem—one that we'll never overcome if we continue to ignore and run from it?

Below is a list of ways we can begin to work together and get to the root of our issues:

- Become aware of all the things we have in common instead of focusing on differences.

- Look at each other as one and not the enemy.

- Support black businesses.

- Work together as families and communities to solve issues.

The more you know what needs to be done in your neighborhoods and towns, the better decisions you'll be able to make toward creating a successful and peaceful community. One of the keys is to keep the police out of your communities so we can stop being harmed by them. Making our communities free of violence is a lot to ask, but it's the only way we can keep the police from snuffing out black lives.

Why is it that wealthy neighborhoods see less violence? Are those neighborhoods better than anyone else's? Is it that only the finest people get to live in those neighborhoods? No, it's because of a difference in mentality. Wealthy people take pride in their environment and look out for one another, which is something seriously missing from black communities and low-income neighborhoods. We can't stop our suffering unless we stop running from the truth. If we continue to run from the truth, we won't do anything to spark change in our neighborhoods.

We don't even talk to our neighbors. Is it because we're afraid of our own people? Have we bought into the hype that the black youth of today are out of control, aggressive, and violent? Why are so many of us allowing others to define who we are? Are many black people ignorant to the physical and psychological attack on them, and therefore don't know how to block out the negative images that are portrayed of them on a constant basis? We must do more than just march to stop the violence. It's time that we all wake up to what needs to be done. I'm here to spread love, but what is love in black communities today? What does that word stand for? Why is it only used outside of our neighborhoods, and not within? If we take the time to focus on what's happening, we can be more understanding of how our young people are feeling and their perspective of the world. We must do more than complain. We need to step up and assist those who need our help. If we don't act, we'll continue to suffer as the rest of the world looks on in silence. But this is our problem, and we can't afford to turn our heads to the violence any longer. Can you envision change taking place in your community, or are you content with just sitting back and complaining about what other people are doing wrong in your eyes? Things can get better, but it starts with each one being a catalyst for change. The turmoil you're experiencing in your neighborhood won't magically go away. You must do something to stop it.

For too long, the way we've dealt with one another hasn't benefited us. Is it any wonder our young people are easy prey for violence within and outside our communities? How can every black man look suspicious in his own neighborhood? How can he be up to something while sitting in front of his house or walking from the store? Why are young black men hunted and killed where they live? Why is it that a group of black young men walking together is seen completely different from a group of young white males? The way black men are automatically viewed as criminals must stop, and everyone who takes part in perpetuating this perspective must be held accountable for their actions.

Below is a list of things that people in black communities need to focus on:

- Create mentorship and tutoring programs.

- Create programs to protect youths that want to remove themselves from gang life.

- Get knowledge of self and share that with your people.

- Get rid of the drug houses and create programs and safe havens where drug users can recover.

- Stand up for yourself and your people.

It would benefit all of us if we came together to make a difference in our communities. Collectively, we can develop and implement solutions to the troubling occurrences we experience. We all have the power to create change, and we should stop looking for a certain leader to do all the work for us. Each of us plays a key role in the upliftment of black people. We must work to make sure that black neighborhoods aren't war zones, and we can do that by helping each other see that violence is counterproductive. We shouldn't only be concerned about getting ours and forget everyone else. Everyone looking out for each other with an unselfish mentality will benefit the whole and create a peaceful existence.

Many say that young black men are a menace to society, but I beg to differ because another race has defined them as such, and I refuse to accept that label. To eliminate the violence and hopelessness, we must first change how we see each other. Self-hate must become self-love to create a peaceful and prosperous world for black people.

CHAPTER EIGHT

ARE WE SABOTAGING OUR COMMUNITIES?

Our black neighborhoods are dying, and the young people are taking the blame for it. The time for pointing fingers is over, and the time for action is here. We're not only losing our youth, but we're also losing our elders due to abandonment and lack of care. Why are we acting in a way that benefits the system of white supremacy? We're stronger that we believe we are, and our voices will have a major impact if we can come together.

Why do we sabotage our efforts when we start to make progress? Why are our children the victims of drive-bys and hate crimes within our communities? Why, because we allow it, and we've decided to put the blame on them instead of taking responsibility for our part in this madness. Black-on-black violence is nothing new, and in fact, it's one of many tactics used to cause our annihilation. We must wake up and see this. Amid our in-fighting, a sinister plan is successfully being carried out, but we're too busy hating ourselves and trying to appease white people that we're blind to it.

When things go wrong, we tear down our own neighborhoods, and many of our black neighborhoods in the United States resemble third world countries. Why aren't the men and elders in the community standing up instead of letting our youth and women fight this battle alone? This isn't the time to take a break. We must all do something because racism isn't going anywhere until we put it to death. Sabotaging our neighborhoods while we encounter a lack of justice, leaves many of us stunned and helpless. How can we lessen the amount of crime and violence in our neighborhoods? When no one is willing to fight for change, it makes people feel helpless and trapped. The worst of it all is when you try to make a difference and the people you expect to help end up sabotaging your plans and contributing to the community's demise.

Below are the factors that if improved, will help us work together and make progress:

- Communication.

- Each person take responsibility for the state of black America and play a role in change and upliftment.

- Respect and love yourself and other black people.

- Take care of the mentality and actions of yourself and your family before telling others what they need to do.

Many black neighborhoods have become war zones that resemble poverty-stricken countries, and when these images are flashed on the news, they're horrible to watch. Let's start cleaning up where we live and beautifying our blocks. Most youths aren't gangbangers because they want to be. They've been forced into that life because they had no one else that cared about them. When a child seeks guidance and there's none there, they'll create an environment where they feel some type of love and attention, even if it's pseudo-love and destructive attention. What environment have you allowed to be created for your family? The fact that you can see what's going on around you means you have another opportunity to spark change.

As you can see, we have a fight on our hands, and we've chosen to attack each other instead of putting that energy on the real enemy. For racism to thrive, one race has to psychologically hate itself, then physical destruction will inevitably follow.

How long can we survive with this way of thinking

and behaving? Are we too far gone to be helped? I

believe that it's never too late to reverse negativity.

But if you're waiting for someone from the outside

to come save you, you'll be waiting an eternity.

You're looking at your savior in the mirror and in

our fellow brothers and sisters. We have the power

to turn our situation around and we're the ones who

will have to make it happen. Looking for a handout

from the white man is a waste of time and energy.

I've learned that the worst thing about not having

enough time to do something positive is knowing

that I had plenty of opportunities to get started

earlier. Start now. Make a change now, and stop

putting it off for some future date. We don't need

organizations or appointed leaders to tell us what to do. We already have all the answers and abilities within us.

I understand that chaos can breed extreme conditions, and many in those conditions have become immune to their environment as others watch in horror. It's time to wake up and do something about your treacherous situation? It's true that nothing gets better overnight, but nothing will ever get better if no one takes that first step. Everything that happens bad in a black community isn't because of black-on-black crime. It's much bigger than that. Let's not forget that the media has no issues with perpetuating the racist and stereotypical views of black people. Does standing up for your community or race make you an activist? No, but it does make you an honorable

human being.

Below is a list that will help change the focus

from negativity to the positive:

- Choose someone to be a spokesperson for

  your neighborhood.

- Get young people involved in community

  decisions.

- Start cleaning your streets and rebuilding

  older homes. Take pride in where you

  reside.

- Talk with people in your neighborhood and

  go to community meetings.

- Teach those around you how to overcome struggle and turn it into a positive.

Who wants to live in a world where you're looked down on for how you look, talk, act, and dress, but at the same time those exact things are copied by white people? When you're willing to go along with the demonization of your race, you become a weak-minded follower. When was the last time you took the lead? When was the last time you took a stance? When was the last time you got together with a few on your block and fixed up the neighborhood? Why is it taking you so long to make a difference in your community? Stop battling your neighbors and start uplifting them to create unity.

Even a dog has the sense not to shit or urinate where they sleep? So why are you shitting and urinating on your environment and the people in your neighborhood? Learn how to live peacefully with people that you may disagree with. Learn effective methods of communication instead of killing every time you have a beef with someone. Stop focusing on what you can't do because that only leads to more failure. Whether you think you can or you think you can't, you're right. Once you become aware that you're bigger than your failures, disappointments, pain, and anger, the sooner you can begin to set goals and focus on what you can do to achieve them. We must first change the way we view ourselves. We should work towards keeping crime out of our neighborhoods while protecting our women, children, and elderly. When we make sure that all children have a support system, there won't be a need for gangs any longer.

When are we going to begin making a positive impact on one another's lives instead of using violence and hate to tear each other down? In the end, when you destroy your communities because you don't like a verdict or because you're unhappy with how the police behave in your neighborhood, you're only destroying yourself. In addition, you're inviting the police and military to come in and do further damage. Let's start using our intellect instead of acting irrationally based on emotions.

CHAPTER NINE

THE HISTORY BEHIND THE DESTRUCTION OF BLACK COMMUNITIES

I've always wondered why we resort to violence when we're unhappy. I can't wrap my mind around the destruction of our own neighborhoods and business. How do we think that destroying what we've built will lead to justice for us? This creates a snowball effect that leads to more of the same injustice and violence that we were upset about in the first place.

Seeing your brother and sister slaughtered in the media is very troubling, but not as troubling as knowing the entire world is witnessing our self-destruction. But who's to blame for these acts of destruction. The world places total blame on the black community, but the bigger question is, why are black people the number one targeted group for discrimination. Why are black neighborhoods the first to go up in smoke? Black communities aren't solely destroyed by black people. There have been many instances when white people burned down our neighborhoods because of pure hate.

Below is a list of times when black communities were targeted by white men because of our success:

- 1863, New York City Draft Riot

- 1906, Atlanta Race Riot

- 1917, The East St. Louis Massacre

- 1919, Chicago Race Riots

- 1919, Washington, D.C. Race Riots

- 1919, Knoxville, Tennessee Race Riots

- 1921, Tulsa, Oklahoma, Black Wall Street

- 1923, Rosewood Massacre

These acts took a toll on these black communities and forced them to start over. Black communities have always been the targets of hate, whether by black hands or white. When you look at the facts, you should ask yourself why you would burn down your own communities when you that was a tactic used *against* us for so long ago. Today, we're still dealing with the burning of black neighborhoods because we're in bondage from mental slavery. The same things that were done to us by outsiders are now being done by the black people within their own communities.

Instead of trying to preserve what we have and help it flourish, we'd rather do the exact thing our oppressor has done to us. Now, history has marked the black man as the one who tears down what little they do have. It's no wonder black people who can afford to move out of black neighborhoods do so.

How many black-owned businesses have been destroyed because of rioting? How many homes and parks have been destroyed because of the constant violence and destruction? When will this destructive behavior be turned into building?

To understand why something is the way it is, you must deal with the cause and not the effects. But very few want to go back far enough to see when these despicable acts began and why only black neighborhoods are affected? It's like white American has voluntary amnesia as they've chosen to forget the days when their ancestors would destroy our new cars, farmland, and businesses. Now they've spun the narrative as if blacks have always been savages that destroy our own. Why are we still being steered in the wrong direction when it comes to history and facts? When we look at the history of black communities going up in flames, we're somehow always taken back to the Watts riots, August 11-17, 1965. Why won't this America look at how, why, and when the black communities were even introduced to this idea. If you look hard enough, you will see how this all began and how it was taught to a generation of people who are tired, frustrated, and angry due to lack of job opportunities and dismal living conditions. Over time, many generations have been affected by such attacks, and the looters have found some sort of satisfaction in destroying their own environment since they feel powerless to handle the injustices they face on a daily basis.

We must now find a way to turn away from what was introduced to us many years ago. The time has come for everyone in our communities to stand up and let your brothers know that you'll no longer accept the destruction of your neighborhoods as a statement against inequality and injustice. Turn your rage into an intelligence that will allow you to come up with a plan to help black people to succeed and flourish. Transform the negative into a positive. Do you hear the call to unify with your brethren? The joke is on you and the community that you love. It's funny how what we claim to cherish and respect each other, but we're cruel and disrespectful towards one another.

There are countless situations where our peaceful marches became violent because of the police, but that seems to be overlooked in the media. What we've failed to realize is that there's never a peaceful march when it comes to the black community. Destruction waits in many forms to create a hell that we're always forced to rebuild. As we should see by now, marching isn't making a difference in the well-being of black America. It's doing nothing to bring about change in our communities. It only allows others to take pleasure in our anger and hurt being displayed all over the world. The world has continually seen us pick up the torch to destroy our own neighborhoods. Stop and think about what you're accomplishing and who's benefits when you tear down your neighborhoods. The residual effect is the continued economic poverty because businesses won't want anything to do with your community after seeing you destroy it out of rage.

Today is the day you must begin to pick up the pieces and hold yourself responsible for playing into the hands of racism through violence toward your brother and sisters and destruction of black-owned businesses. You're not a savage as the media portrays you. Turn the TV off, get knowledge of self, and find out who you really are and your true potential. Rise from the ashes and refuse to be defeated. Use your minds and voices to make change.

CHAPTER TEN

SELF-DISCRIMINATION

It seems that after a black man became

President, things took a turn for the worst, and black

people became mentally lazy as if we had 'arrived'

somehow. No one seemed to make the connection

that black murders by the hands of white men

increased because we had a black president. More

needed to be done toward the progression of black

people. We made a mistake by becoming content

with having a black man in the Oval Office as if all our problems were solved because of it.

We must do more than just march and sing songs. We need to stand together and learn from previous black communities that supported each other economically and educationally. A people divided cannot stand, and they're destined to fail. As much as we don't want to face it, only when we see young black people executed in the streets do we decide to come together and sing songs of unity and harmony. Who are you fooling? You are the same people who passed a black man or woman on the street, in the store, or at the job and didn't speak, but you made sure to speak to a white coworker or stranger. This is a dangerous game we play. We're practicing self-discrimination and self-hate. It's your choice if you want to behave this way, but don't scream injustice when you're disrespected or passed over for a job by the same people you rushed to be friendly with over your fellow black brother or sister.

We must learn to love ourselves if we want to be respected. We still look at each other as competition instead of being happy for and supporting one another. We have patience for everyone except those who look like us. Why is this? Why do we trust our oppressor over each other? We can't better ourselves if we're too afraid to confront those issues that are killing us like a cancer. For change to occur, we'll have to come together. We've allowed ourselves to be divided and defined by titles, degrees, religion, and status.

Our perception of each other is sick, yet we take no responsibility for our demise. How many times have you thought very little of the black person that works or lives next to you? Have you compared yourself to them in a competitive manner? Why are we so hard on our own? There are no simple answers to these questions because we're dealing with psychological training that was implanted during slavery.

Below is a list of ways black people interact with each other negatively that causes division:

- Anti-social toward other blacks.

- Disloyal.

- Disrespectful towards each other, but respectful towards white people.

- Judgmental.

- Rejection.

- Neglect.

As I look at how we as a race have been divided and conquered, it hurts my heart. The way we can begin to work together is to understand that other black people aren't the enemy. We must make this decision on our own because it's not going to be taught by the school system, in the media, or in the workplace. Black people need to start learning to educate themselves instead of waiting on white people to tell them what's important. We've become so disconnected that this distance has taken over in our communities and homes. No wonder so many black lives are taken by police. Because we're divided, we don't have the power to enforce consequences or put pressure on the judicial system to deliver justice. There's absolutely no strength in division. We're such a lost group that the only time we want to fight for each other's lives is when someone outside of our race takes a black life. What about the many young people that die by our hands daily? What about the high crime rate in our cities that we've caused? It's no wonder other groups see our neighborhoods as killing grounds?

Why are we so mad when the life of our youth is taken by law enforcement? Why do we care? When are we going to wake up and put a stop to all the killings that take place in the black community at the hands of a black man? The mainstream focus is on law enforcement killing black unarmed black people, but what about when we kill each other? We are yet to discuss all the lives snuffed out at the hands of our own. Aren't those lives precious, too? Killing or shooting someone is wrong no matter who pulls the trigger. Why aren't we talking about this more? If we are to stop the loss of black life, we must also bring attention to the blood that's on our hands as well. We can't change the public view of us if we don't first change how we view and treat each other.

Are we ready for change or do we just want to march to appear to look concerned? Are we going to continue to only be outraged when black people are murdered by white hands? The public execution of all black life must stop, even at the hands of our own. We must start to show the world that we care for our own and that we have no problem protecting our own. When the world sees this type of unity, they'll be less likely to show up in our neighborhoods with reckless killing and unjust treatment. We decide how we're treated by the value we see in each other. The way to end self-discrimination is through self-knowledge and self-love.

CHAPTER ELEVEN

BREAKING OUT OF CHAOS

The mass murdering of our youth in plain sight is a battle that my grandparents had to deal with, and it's still going on today. This chaos should make us want to do more to eliminate the fear and death that permeates the streets. Instead of ending this craziness, we live with it. We have the mindset that we don't have the power to make change because we're not politicians or wealthy. But there's strength in numbers, and if we unify, we'll have all the power we need to destroy the system of

racism white supremacy. Not only does the world

judge us, but we also judge each other, and the

fighting within our own communities must end. The

keys to life and knowledge-of-self are within each

of us, but we continue to look for answers from

outside ourselves. We need to learn to work

together despite any differences in political views or

religion. When we get knowledge of self, we'll be

able to embrace our innate beauty, strength, and

uniqueness. Each of us has a duty to stand up for

our human rights.

How do we stop the killing of our youth? We

police our own neighborhoods. The question is,

how many of us are willing to consistently take on

that responsibility. How many of us must be killed

before we demand justice? We all see the crime, but where is the punishment? Who will pay for these killings besides the families of the slaughtered? You're experiencing chaos, and chaos has one purpose—destruction. How do you calm the tears of the mother and father that have lost a child? What could you possibly say to ease the pain in their hearts? Why are we being sacrificed daily? How can we start anew? What is my brother's or sister's struggle? How can I help them? Are we too cowardice to help our own people? Why have we allowed our children to continue to fight this four-hundred-year-old battle while doing nothing to help them understand why things are the way they are? Are sports the only escape from poverty, death, and incarceration for our young men? What are you doing to make change for your community? Stop being afraid to stand up for what's right, and do something that will help the people in your community.

Below is a list of ways to create safe neighborhoods:

- Create an 1-800 hotline where crime can be reported anonymously.

- Create safehouses for young people who are being bullied or abused.

- Have weekly or monthly meetings to discuss how the community will police themselves.

Peace is needed if we're to move forward, and the real war isn't your brother or sister, but the unjust legal system that we've been brainwashed to believe in. That system is just as broken as the rest of the world. Real change is fostered by understanding, and the legal system has made no attempts to understand black people. We must show love and understanding to each other and take the responsibility of creating justice in our communities. No one can know our neighborhoods better than we do. With that knowledge, how are you going to spark change? It won't happen overnight, but eventually the police presence in our neighborhoods will cease because they won't be needed. We'll be policing ourselves. That's how we end the public executions of black men and women.

You don't need to fear any man, but we must learn how to remove people that are threats to our safety and well-being. If you don't understand the planned chaos that has taken over the black community, then you're not mentally prepared to be in this fight for your life. You're not ready to do what it takes to live in peace and prosperity. We are attracting the same chaos that we are issuing on each other daily. The chaos will stop when we stop looking for the people who created the chaos to solve our problems.

It feels as if only racist people have joined the police force, and the few good cops are greatly outnumbered by their evil counterparts. Evil can never be completely removed in a duality-based existence, but you can make yourself aware of how to change your vibration to limit your encounters with evil. Change your focus from what "they" are doing to what *you* can do to shape your reality to one that is harmonious. The more we focus on "them", the less we focus on our own actions and the more brutality we'll continue to experience because what you focus on expands.

When I hear people talk about letting someone else come in and teach them how to act civilized, all I can do is shake my head in disgust because as original people, no one from the outside has to show you how to conduct yourself. You taught the world science, mathematics, and how to live harmoniously with nature and people. Physical slavery may have ended, but our minds are still bound by psychological locks and chains. That's displayed every day with how we treat each other and how we look for a white savior to solve our problems and show us the way.

Until we look at the genuine issues that are impacting our neighborhoods, nothing will ever change. Change takes focus, effort, and the ability to strategize your way through problematic circumstances. Which one of you is up for this challenge. It has nothing to do physical fighting, but using our minds to out-think our opponent. Brute force has nothing to do with making a difference. We need to become intellectual and spiritual masterminds. We must begin to deal with first cause, which is the spirit and the mind. Those two create the objective reality you see, and only by dealing with cause can you change effects. Never the other way around. Now you can see why marching, shooting, and looting have done nothing in the way of progress. Take back your power by removing fear from your hearts. Fear gives your circumstance control over you. Your fear and anger only fuel the machine and put you further into bondage. This isn't about marching or protesting, but instead a change in consciousness.

CHAPTER TWELVE

IT STARTS WITH US

Before you can right any wrong or seek justice

for it, you must see if you're the one causing the

issues that are affecting you. You want the killings

and executions to stop, but you're acting the same

way with your own people. You find the killing of

black people wrong when a white person does it, yet

it appears that black life doesn't matter to black

people, because if it did, we wouldn't kill each

other and no one would be able to come into our neighborhoods and wreak havoc. The battle to end the mass killings of black life starts at home. If you don't value black life, why should anyone else.

Use your mind to make a difference. Do you really need someone to tell you how to think? How many more lives must be eliminated before something is done? Do you really think this mess is all just going to blow over, and you miraculously wake up to peace, love, and respect? If you do, then you're in a poor mental state. You must be willing to put in the work to get the outcome you desire. That goes for anything, and justice is no exception. Enough is enough, and accountability must be taken for the black blood that has been spilled around the world.

It sickens me that we've become blind to what's going on because of our hate for each other. That hate is just one more thing that makes the world look at us in disgust. We must take accountability for the state we're in. We all want this chaos that dominates our lives to end, but for that to occur, we must put aside petty differences and work together as a collective to make it happen. We have more power together than we ever will divided. Instead of waiting on someone else to improve our economic state, we should educate ourselves and make it happen. We're like students that only read the content that the teacher instructs us to. We don't see the importance of taking the initiative to be self-educated. A system that wants to see your demise will only teach you how to uphold its system and create your own demise.

Below is a list of things that black people must account for:

Blaming the youth for all issues.

Broken homes where the father isn't present.

Chasing fame and materialism instead of health and generational wealth.

Content with being over-worked on a 9-5 job and lacking entrepreneurial spirit.

Division between younger and older generations.

Individualistic and selfish mindset.

Lack of respect for elders.

Lack of mentorship for youth by the elders.

Moral degradation.

Refusing to read, which has led to a lack knowledge and spiritual development.

Change takes willingness to focus, sacrifice, and take responsibility for the predicament you're in. Only a shift in consciousness will enable you to take the steps that will lead to a rise from the ashes.

Our communities have been taken over by criminals and drug lords from within, which sends the message to outsiders that we don't value ourselves and they're free to do what they want to us. Our young people have no respect for authority or elders, and the elders in turn, don't respect the youth. Each of us must take the first step to end this cycle and stop waiting for someone else to make the first move. We are all leaders in our own right, so stop looking for someone to follow.

Organization is something that's absent from the black community, but it's a necessity for us to thrive. We need to start using the power of our minds to change our circumstances and end the madness! No one should be able to turn you against your brother or sister and disrespect them. If you don't control your own mind, someone else will and someone else has been for many years. We must start loving each other and believing in one another. We need to start seeing each other as the beautiful and golden souls that we are.

Let's learn from the history of the 1920's with Black Wall Street. We had our own businesses, banks, schools and law enforcement. The only hate and negativity that surrounded us was outside of our communities. We no longer know what it is to work together, and this mindset is dangerous and counterproductive. Can we make a difference in the lives of other black people? The answer is yes, if we build from within instead of seeking outsiders to handle our affairs.

We must turn away from the mindsets of poverty, jealousy, anger, fear, suffering, and struggle before we can experience peace, love, happiness, health, and wealth. Alter your consciousness to change your reality. This is a call for you to spiritually awaken so you can mold your physical reality into a prosperous and harmonious state. WAKE UP!!!